Words and Whisky

Sidney Coe

BookLeaf Publishing

Presentation by *BookLeaf Publishing*

Web: www.bookleafpub.com

E-mail: info@bookleafpub.com

ISBN: 9789357212441

First edition 2023

DEDICATION

To Cathy, our Breath of Spring.

PREFACE

Nothing is ever known until it is known for the first time. An awareness that even the ordinary and mundane can elicit a sense of awe and excitement as everyone has the opportunity to discover everything for the first time, unencumbered by prediction or anticipation. The meaning of life is life. The magic of life is awe. The purpose of life is to be useful. Enjoy.

The Web

Entries in the Archibald are painted portraits on a wall.
The famous faces we recall do not really tell us all
we need to know about who they are or what they did or how they think.
Lines of paint capture light and colour. I use paper, pen and ink
to capture time between these lines. Spinnerets inside my head
like a spiders golden web, spun with words of silk instead.
To entrap in its sticky thread all I felt and thought and said.
Immobilised. Unfrozen when the moment is relived reread.

Thinking.

Ticking. Ticking.
I can hear the old clock ticking
and like the thoughts that I am thinking
in the silence both seem loud.

While logic, wheels of logic
turn, and thoughts and hands keep pace.
Paths that both in sequence trace
are neither simple nor profound.

But revolving keep evolving.
From a thought, a new thought born.
We're to new horizons drawn
or precedent recall

within the realm of reason.
Responses varied and diverse
are unceasing in their search
for answers. Some are found

while most remain unsolved.
Failure does not mean defeat.
Logic's metronomic beat
knows no other sound.

Thoughts turn in a full circle
to the point where once begun.
Hands divergent rejoin one.
Like the clock upon the wall
Ticking.

Words and Whisky

Writing poetry is risky,
when I'm also drinking whisky.
Even though the demon drink
disinhibits what I think
and thoughts aglow, the words will flow.
Good or bad, who's to know?

One thing though is assured
As certain, with the next shot poured
if words come less and whisky more,
I find myself upon the floor
worse for wear, from the night before.

Hemmingway said to write pissed
and edit sober. Less is missed,
when by chance the words come first
and I somehow quench the thirst.
Through the vapours then might creep
a thought of worth that I can keep.

My father's name

In the name of the father and the son.
Holy spirit. Three are one
when what my father once taught me
I in turn now teach my son
Like a wheel that slowly turns.
Another cycle has begun.

What I mean is what I say.
What I say will be done.
In the kingdom of the mind
three generations rein as one.
An identity the crown,
sought and found, lost or won,
from the lessons we have learned
and the races we have run.

As a new day somewhere dawns
from the setting of the sun
what my father means to me
is the man that I become.

To The Brave

Halfway down Alexandra Street
Where the past and present meet
There stands an obelisk of stone
Within the scene it stands alone
Silent in its memory save
For these three words "To The Brave".

Anzac Day

Old soldiers march on Anzac Day in columns six abreast
with pride and youthful vigour, blazing medals on their chest,
to honour fallen comrades and their deeds of valour Lest
We Forget our dead. The Fallen. Even though we may detest
the price old men make their youths pay appeasing Gods of War.
To think how many lives were lost. The days they never saw
or surviving it, left scarred. As the columns pass before,
what motivates these men to march like enlisted troops once more?
To honour youth and courage. Those forever young we're told
shall not let aging weary them as we who live grow old
and selfish when the selfless served and died. The life they sold
for lines of gilt-edged glory in ornately lettered gold.

While flags forlornly flutter in remembrance at half mast
the crowd stand still and silent while the bugler plays the Last
Post in respect for those who died. The mourners filing past
the cenotaph bear witness to the countless actors cast
in plays with opaque plots. The rough and reckless, brave and bold
who were then asked to surrender their brief and fragile hold
on their present for our future when in future we behold
the issues long forgotten once the cannon mouths were cold.

Generations with a debt would forget the men who bled
for a cause unless we pause this day. Our eyes would never shed
tears of remorse for the fallen and the lives they never led
unless this ritual was repeated. Yearly oaths and rites reread.
So old soldiers march on Anzac Day for it never to be said
that men died in vain for a cryptic cause, misguided or misled.
Their names are all recorded and are yearly somewhere read.
One line of guilt edged glory in memory of the dead.

The Mirror Maze

We walk within a mirror maze. The images we see
amuse us as we take our turn. What hides the passage free
are reflections of ourselves. And many lose their way,
misled by mirrors in our minds that tempt us all to stray.
Confused are they who come to some abrupt and blind dead end
yet faithful to appearances in fantasy defend
that which another says they see must be a measure true
of who you are and what you're worth reflecting back at you.
But mirrors can be made to make us seem what we are not.
They tell us we possess the things we want and haven't got
and those who see themselves through another person's eyes
will see their worth with opinion, change and still be no more wise.

It's not until we see beyond the boundary of our face
that we make sense of what we see, and wayward steps retrace.
For when our eyes no longer see reflections, we begin
to see what lies behind the mask. We find the wealth within.
And though none can forever pass a point of no return,
answers only come to those who ask questions. We can learn
if we lose our way within this maze and images confound,
to not look in the mirror but more closely at the ground.
For there a path, the track well worn, lies etched upon the floor
whereon the wise in days gone by passed along before.
So pay no head to what you see reflected round about.
There is a path from chaos that with faith will lead you out.

Happiness

We've been given one command
to try and love our fellow man
and though I do not understand
the how or why or eternal plan
I do know this
that happiness
is loving you.

The Vow

The day,
the dress,
the cake,
the kiss
celebrating wedded bliss
and the moment that exists
to mark the union that it is.

But of one thing we can be sure.
moments merge into years. And for
the unsuspecting human heart
we grow together or apart
when time and circumstances pull
at our intentions. Purposeful
are the couples who can say
I love you more than I did this day.

They say "I love you" and
"You love me" too.
Over and over and over because
the vow
is a wish
that repeated
comes true.

Eight Archers

They dress in skin-tight thermals and threadbare mismatched socks
when "hands across the boat" chirps the ever-cheerful cox
and the morning lights first feeble rays, in search of day, pierce through
the rising mist. A city sleeps; the sun will greet this crew.

None fear the cold discomfort. They're immune now to its bite
and ensuing work will warm them. While in the morning light
still waters form a mirror. In the river they reflect
to form a double image that they practice to perfect.

The puddles pass behind the boat until the smallest swirls
are swallowed in the stillness and as the dawn unfurls
the only imperfection on the surface of the lake
is a tiny ripple, testament to this living quarrel's wake.

Backs brace like an archers bow. With grace and tensile ease
this bolt of eight young athletes is launched in harmonies
of co-ordinated movement. The boat runs straight and true
when eight combine their power and become as one a crew

With every act a copy of the pattern set by Stroke.
Muscles gnarled and knotted strain beneath their yoke
and sitting back, with smooth release, unleash the force applied
while in synchrony blades feather as they roll onto their side

To the rhythm of the Stroke. The oar, a sweeping swallow,
skims the lake; at equal height another seven follow.
With balance and precision that is felt more than is seen
eight feathered blades in unison leave the water clean.

And level hands maintain control easing down the Slide.
Beneath the boat the water sings. Recovering, they glide
to close the angles, force compressed. Recoiling at the Catch
that without a wasted movement is sprung in sharp dispatch

As the clip of eight bright blades resounds as one around the bay

when the oars lock in united to send her on her way.
Accelerating rapidly the boats alacrity
belies the strength required and how painful that can be.

For they train to race. They train to win, and their patience is repaid
when they come before the starter's gun. In flight the flashing blade
needs quick acceleration and a rate of forty-two
commands complete control of every trained and tense sinew.

They race two thousand meters in five minutes. At these speeds
equal strength and stamina are what each oarsman needs
and as the hungry bows divide and scythe in two the course
the fuel to feed the fury is the maximum of force.

Imagine if you can the pace as six crews race and how
with the finish fast approaching your opponents push their bow
half a length ahead. The Stroke will pass them if he can
by rating even higher, and straining to a man

they lunge toward the finish line oblivious to pain
with nothing left to lose and much in winning gain.
A merciful exhaustion overwhelms at races end
as agonising breaths on tired weary men descend.

The winner's quick recovery, their weariness soon past,
will leave unwanted pain the fate of those who are outclassed.
To the victor goes the honour while the vanquished weakly toss
their vessel from the water and bear them like a cross.

The burden weighs on shoulders and their faces show dismay
accepting the defeat. They know there is no other way
except to train and toil on the water every dawn.
A morning homage to the sun until success is born.

So, if you ever rise before the birds and chance to see
eight archers launch their quarrel, to pierce serenity,
it's a daily rite repeated and a price that they will pay
in pursuit of their perfection, and to race another day.

This Land

I acknowledge the traditional custodians of this land and its elders past, present & emerging.

Let me paint for you a landscape with words. About a land
where the waves are never-ending and pine trees proudly stand.
Where islands in three oceans forged this southern nation and
ringed with gold is boldly crowned by wind-blown sun-bleached sand.

Where quanta of each crystal quartz, first in a breaker borne
are thrown back against the shores from whence they once were torn
to weave its crown from weathered rock. Wild waters are the host
in which a beach is born and cast in fury to the coast.

A land where tides hide treasures from the deep. A shell, a pearl
from the vast eternal ocean where endless breakers curl
and the pounding of the surf upon the seashore, like a heart,
is the essence of a country sea and time have set apart.

A country changing colour. Unrelenting is the ray
turning newborn buds that once were green, gaunt and lifeless grey.
And tempest tossed the seagulls soar in dark and stormy skies
to guard the windswept whiteness with their eerie piercing cries.

Or the waves' incessant rhythms paint alternating hues
of icy cold foreboding greens and iridescent blues.
And the foam, in white rebellion, is seething to be free
but cannot cut its' shackles to an unforgiving sea.

Where from the surf an on-shore breeze brings sweetly to the nose
the salty scent of sea-spray. Where the sand between your toes
like softly sifted grains of gold are quick in their cascade
to undermine and then erase the mark your passing made.

A land of ancient legend. Where flowing in her veins
are spirits of ancestral sons and daughters. What remains
of an era long forgotten, a dreaming come and gone,
is the sand where myth and magic like the silence linger on.

Where every drop of water has an ocean locked inside
and a rock-pool, as a remnant of the last receding tide,
reflects a mirror image of the sun; where sea and sand
combine to paint a picture of the owners of this land.

Without you what am I?

The tortoise and the turtle both upon a shell rely
to save them when in danger. And grains of wheat and rye
when covered by a kernel as a seed in safety lie.
Yet should we ever take the two and guard from guarded pry
then each without the other would un-needed wilt and die.
As answers need a question, a plane its wings to fly
and mothers need their children, the sun and stars the sky
we all depend on others; needing help to get us by
our trials and tribulations; the demons we defy.
Yet like a land devoid of rain, a desert barren-dry,
some men hard hearted cannot feel and tearless cannot cry
and alone are unfulfilled and incomplete. And that is why
I cannot be without you. For without you what am I?

Joy

It's a joy to me unmeasured when I think of you. I found
all I want and will ever need warmly wrapped around
me and I could not bear to be without. One with whom
I have ceased to play charades as all the faces I assume
to hide true feeling, fall away. To whom to love is not a game
and whose needs and expectations and desires are the same.
Another who will live with me and know and understand
my many moods and feelings. Who makes little her demands
and most her gifts. A gentle teacher and a guide who helped me
learn
how to cherish love. And loved how then to love her in return.

Whose love is fierce and loyal and cannot be won or bought.
Trusted keeper of my secrets who can read my every thought
without a word between us. Who in times of need is there
as my confidant, close companion and my best friend. Who can
share
with me my fortunes and misfortunes, awkward times of doubt and
strife
and still keep smiling. Who can laugh at all the ironies in life
and shrug them off as unimportant. Who will share my ups and
downs
and stand beside me and support me still, when all and sundry
frown
at my mistakes. Who won't desert me when the going gets too
tough
and doesn't want for more but has and sees in me enough.

One who simply with her presence makes my heart inside me
swell.
Who can comfort and console me and make me laugh as well,
making memories that more precious. Who can look at me and tell
me what I am thinking. Cherished more than I care for myself
and for whom I'd do as much as she would do for me, and more,
without a reservation or a need to keep a score.
One with whom the love between us burns, an ever-lasting flame,

forging bonds that can't be broken and that time and fate can't
tame.
One whose needs and expectations and desires are the same
and no longer one apart is one in spirit and in name.

The best thing

The best things in life are not things.
The best things in life don't get old.
Despite all the pleasure and joy that it brings
the best thing in life can't be sold.

It isn't a path or a journey or way.
But there isn't a moment to lose
when it still has a price. And the price that we pay
is something we all get to choose

to spend. It's not free. Even though we forget
or distracted, ignore passing by.
The best thing in life is a gift that we get
from the moment we're born till we die.

The best thing in life are moments like these.
The best thing in my life it's true
are the moments I have and mean most to me.
It's the time that I spend here with you.

Day Pass

Prisons do not all have bars,
And not all walls are brick.
When pain and incapacity
incarcerates the sick.

Trapped inside this dungeon
invariably we find
the chains that bind most tightly
are anchored in the mind.

There often is no answer,
no cure nor a key,
to unlock these chains and shackles.
Setting those who suffer free.

Precious then the moment,
unpardoned on parole,
when wellness feels like freedom
and a Day Pass for the soul.

Driven

Though there is merit in achievement and completing what you
start
there are hazards in becoming too independent. Set apart
by the very set of standards that you think that you require
and pursuing at all costs the destinations you desire.

There is no doubt that good intentions reap us our success
and nothing is ever gained or been achieved of worth unless
we've had them. But at times expectations are not met
when despite our earnest efforts what we want we do not get.

In all things we must try and strike a balance between the two.
To blend the urge to conquer and achievement with a view
to accepting what we find are things we cannot seem to change
or with the skills at our disposal what we seek is out of range.

So, change what can be changed and with determination win
the goals that you have set. And yet forget not to give in
when the task you set is beyond you. There is no shame in defeat
when your effort was your best. Rather, everyone must meet
face to face, their limitations and accept the unknown when
the answer to their question spawns another ten.

The Last Act

The flame of life will flicker when our precious grip, so frail,
weakens in its grasp and our bodies start to fail
beyond the realm of science or a surgeon's futile knife.
The shepherd calls his flock and the winter of our life
will see us wither, waste and wilt like lilies in a pond.
We flower on this earth. How quickly we are gone.
While age appears to many a plight we can't defeat
its victory is hollow, for my memories are sweet
and always will live on of a race superbly run.
In the outcome of the contest, I see it's you who won.

For you bore your loss of function with never much ado
and concern and love for others repeatedly shone through.
If any felt unsettled in your failing fault was theirs
as you had accepted fate with a faith that none compares.
One and all are close to death. It's a fact from which we run
but you faced it as it was and never came undone.
And through that brave acceptance a calm tranquility
was borne upon your face for one and all to see.

Therefore, dear Patricia we can so surely say
this world was all the better for you having passed our way.
And we feel it is a privilege to say that we have known
a lady of great virtue; in your passing we have grown.
You have taught us all a lesson with serene simplicity
that the only way to live is with grace and dignity.
And all I wish conveyed by this simple sad oration
is that we should realize you deserve a grand ovation.
Even though we mourn the loss of a mother, friend and wife
we salute the courage shown in your last great act of life.

Did I tell you?

I don't tell you enough that I love you.
When last did I say that I care?
From the soles of your feet that I massage
at night. To the tips of the locks of your hair.

Did I tell you how much I need you?
How my lonely heart just follows
wherever your life may lead you.
Yesterday, today and tomorrow.

Did I tell you how much I miss you
Every time you walk out the door?
And the thrill that I feel when I kiss you
When you reappear once more.

Like a fish in a bowl that forgets
every time that it circles around.
I don't tell you enough that you ground me.
I do know that love can compound.

I can't tell you enough that I love you.
Even though its my mantra I find
too much still falls short and once more
is once less than I have on my mind.

The Sanctuary

There is a place where I can go
That only I alone would know
How to get to. To rest, to dream
When all is not as it would seem
and noise beyond does not relent.
A place of quiet calm content.

If "Greed is Good" but cant fulfil,
why do the rich seek riches still?
If won with work but kept in fear
lest others dare to venture near
and see success so keenly sought
is hollow and account for naught.

Signs say life is lust and pleasure.
Thrill a number and a measure
of our value. Or when we steal
without a care because we feel
a quest for more. And then of course
impose our will on all by force.

Words of wisdom have decreed
there is no need to flaunt a deed
or place for lies and false pretense.
No waspish tongue to cause offence
and image worship is insane;
insatiable, forever vain.

For we have much and need no more.
And we are rich. We are not poor
and do not take but learn to give.
The difference is we learn to live
than just exist. Tranquility
is wealth enough. Love's purity,
respect and harmony entwined,
are congruent and unconfined.

So resolutely I defend
my mental health. Repair and mend
whenever worldly egos breach.
I guard against the taint and reach
and fear no foe nor shun a friend.
And fear not death. The trials end
when all I wish for in this life
amid the noise and haste and strife
is to maintain the peace I find
within the shelter of my mind.

Passing Time

Passing time at Wylie's Baths
The waves beyond a pond of glass
Ripples as the swimmers pass
Back and forth. Came and went.

Floating then in Gordon's Bay.
Coloured fish dart and play
Among the rocks and fronds that sway.
Tassels that the tides torment.

Strolling in Centennial Park
Bikes and horses kept apart
By lines and lanes of trees and cars.
Parades of people. A movement

that merrily around it goes.
Time is life. We ebb and flow
And in that moment come to know
That passing time is time well spent.

These Words

Time is a thief and as the seconds pass events
are easily forgotten. Lost, unless we have the sense
to lock the fleeting moments of these precious passing days
within a verse or sentence. Captured in a phrase
before it slips into the abyss of the unremembered. Most
of my memories are not immortal. I write to hold and host
the present that is passing and I desire not destroyed
or beyond the realm of recall lost in time's eternal void.
So I write. Not for another when not many will agree
with how I think and what I say. I write these lines for me.
To keep account of what occurred and how my life has changed.
I try and snare the seconds of existence. And I aim
to paint as any artist captures mood in form and line,
with words. To conjure pictures in the corner of my mind
of places, people, feeling, things I've thought and could not say
uniquely felt for the first time, wrote down and put away
to guard against the minutes as they march. To then one day
reread and recollect that once I felt a certain way
or had a certain thought. And in comparing Now and Then,
lessons learned are relearned when my memories live again.
And I care not for another's cold opinion of my prose.
I require no critique when all the things expressed are those
that mean most to me. No matter how absurd they may appear,
these words flow freely from my pen, are pleasant to my ear
and need no other judge.

www.ingramcontent.com/pod-product-compliance
Lightning Source LLC
Chambersburg PA
CBHW062110140826
49812CB00058B/1213
* 9 7 8 9 3 5 7 2 1 2 4 4 1 *